READING POWER

19th Century American Inventors

The Inventions of

Thomas Alva Edison

Father of the Light Bulb and the
Motion Picture Camera

Holly Cefrey

The Rosen Publishing Group's
PowerKids Press™
New York

Published in 2003 by The Rosen Publishing Group, Inc.
29 East 21st Street, New York, NY 10010

First Edition

Book Design: Daniel Hosek

Photo Credits: All images appear courtesy of U.S. Department of the Interior, National Park Service, Edison National Historic Site

Library of Congress Cataloging-in-Publication Data

Cefrey, Holly.
The inventions of Thomas Alva Edison : father of the light bulb and the motion picture camera / Holly Cefrey.
    p. cm. — (19th century American inventors)
Summary: Provides a biographical sketch of Thomas Alva Edison and a description of some of his most important inventions.
Includes bibliographical references and index.
ISBN 0-8239-6440-X (library binding)
1. Edison, Thomas A. (Thomas Alva), 1847-1931—Juvenile literature.
2. Inventors—United States—Biography—Juvenile literature. [1. Edison, Thomas A. (Thomas Alva), 1847-1931. 2. Inventors.] I. Title. II. Series.
TK140.E3 C34 2003
621.3'092—dc21

                                             2002000106

Contents

Young Thomas Edison

Thomas Alva Edison was one of the greatest inventors in history. He was born in Milan, Ohio, on February 11, 1847. He was the seventh and youngest child of Samuel and Nancy Edison.

Edison's mother, Nancy, was a former teacher.

Edison went to school for only a few months. Because his teachers thought that he was a slow learner, Edison's mother taught him at home.

This photo shows Edison at about the age of four.

The Fact Box

Young Edison was nicknamed Al from his middle name Alva.

Edison enjoyed learning about science. He liked to do experiments. Edison built working models of a sawmill and a railroad engine. They were both powered by steam.

When he was fifteen, Edison got a job working a telegraph. Even with hearing problems, Edison became good at his job.

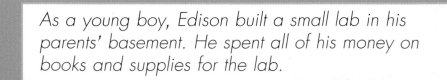

As a young boy, Edison built a small lab in his parents' basement. He spent all of his money on books and supplies for the lab.

Thomas Edison at age 14

The Home of Great Ideas

In 1876, Edison built a lab that was known as the invention factory, in Menlo Park, New Jersey. There, he began work that would change the world. Edison promised that he would turn out a minor invention every ten days and a big invention every six months.

Edison and his workers have their picture taken at the Menlo Park lab.

"I find out what the world needs, then I go ahead and try to invent it."
—Thomas Edison

The Fact Box

Edison only slept four to five hours a night. But he often napped in his office.

Inventions That Changed the World

In 1877, Edison invented the phonograph. His phonograph recorded sound on a piece of tinfoil and then played it back. Later, phonographs would play records.

Edison formed the Edison Speaking Phonograph Company to sell his machine.

FORM NO. 392

THE Edison PHONOGRAPH

EDISON TRIUMPH PHONOGRAPH

UNCLE SAM TAKES OFF HIS HAT.

THE TRIUMPH $50.00

NONE GENUINE WITHOUT THIS TRADE MARK

Thomas A. Edison

NATIONAL PHONOGRAPH COMPANY

This is a page from Edison's notebook. He drew this picture of his phonograph before he built it.

Edison's original tinfoil phonograph

"Of all my inventions, I like the phonograph best."
—Thomas Edison

In 1879, Edison invented a long-lasting electric light bulb that could be used in homes. However, not many people could use his new invention. Very few homes or businesses had electricity.

The Fact Box

Edison held 1,093 invention patents. This is more than any other inventor has ever held.

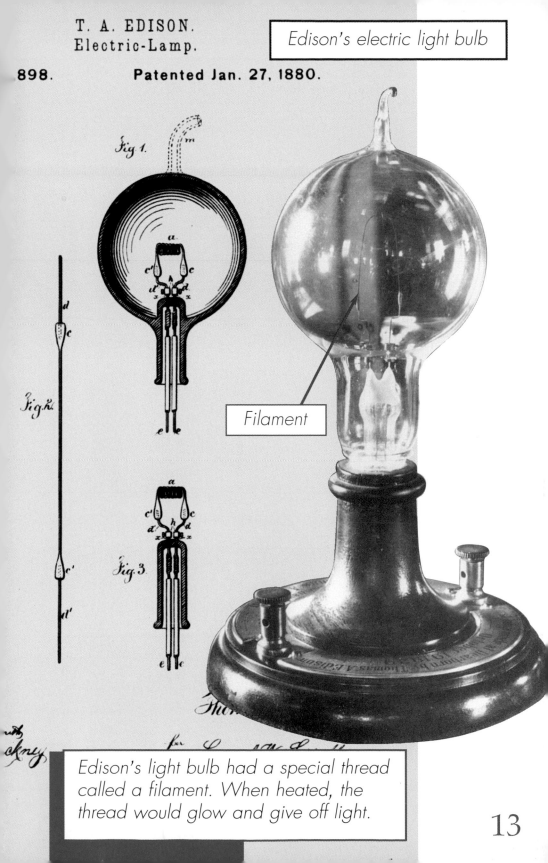

T. A. EDISON.
Electric-Lamp.

898. Patented Jan. 27, 1880.

Fig. 1.

Fig. 2.

Fig. 3.

Edison's electric light bulb

Filament

Edison's light bulb had a special thread called a filament. When heated, the thread would glow and give off light.

Edison invented the electric power system to bring electricity into homes and businesses. By the 1890s, hundreds of towns around the world had Edison power stations.

This is the inside of Edison's first power plant, the Pearl Street Power Station. It was on Wall Street in New York City.

In 1889, Edison invented the Kinetograph, a motion picture camera. The Kinetograph took pictures quickly. The pictures were recorded on a strip of film that was wrapped around a wheel or spool.

Edison had a clear picture of what the Kinetograph could do. He said that the Kinetograph "does for the eye what the phonograph does for the ear."

The Fact Box

Edison started a film studio. The first movie Edison's studio made was *The Sneeze*. It showed an Edison employee, Fred Ott, sneezing.

Edison's Strip Kinetograph

Edison later invented a machine that let people watch the movie. He called it the Kinetoscope. A person could put a coin in the machine and look through a small hole to watch the movie.

The inside of the Kinetoscope had spools through which a strip of film was pulled. When the film was pulled, the pictures looked like they were moving.

Kinetoscope theaters, such as this one, opened up all over the country.

This Kinetophone was Edison's attempt to make movies with sound. The machine did not work well.

The World After Edison

Thomas Edison died on October 18, 1931. Some of his most important inventions helped people spread ideas and information around the world. Edison will always be remembered as someone who put his great ideas to work for everyone.

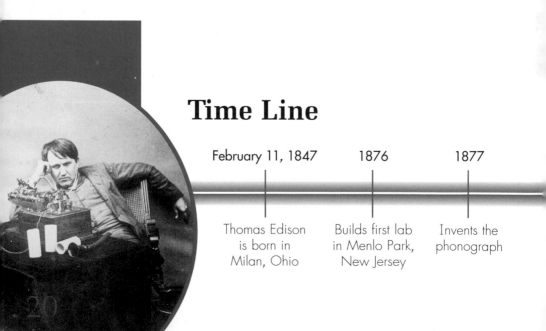

Time Line

February 11, 1847	1876	1877
Thomas Edison is born in Milan, Ohio	Builds first lab in Menlo Park, New Jersey	Invents the phonograph

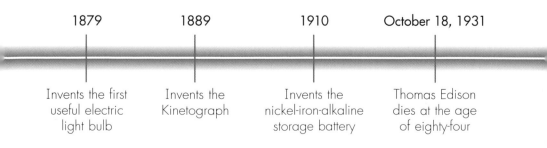

Edison worked hard his whole life.

1879	1889	1910	October 18, 1931
Invents the first useful electric light bulb	Invents the Kinetograph	Invents the nickel-iron-alkaline storage battery	Thomas Edison dies at the age of eighty-four

Glossary

electricity (ih-lehk-**trihs**-uh-tee) a form of power that is used to make light, heat, or motion

employee (ehm-**ploi**-ee) a person who works for another person or a company

invention (ihn-**vehn**-shuhn) something new that someone thinks of or makes

inventor (ihn-**vehn**-tuhr) a person who thinks of or makes something new

Kinetograph (kuh-**neht**-uh-graf) a camera that records moving pictures

Kinetoscope (kuh-**neht**-uh-skohp) a machine that allows people to watch moving pictures

lab (**lab**) a room or building with special equipment where scientists do tests and experiments

minor (**my**-nuhr) smaller, or less important

patents (**pat**-ehnts) legal papers that give an inventor the rights to make or sell his or her inventions

phonograph (**foh**-nuh-graf) a machine that records and plays sound

studio (**stoo**-dee-oh) a large building or space where movies are made

telegraph (**tehl**-uh-graf) a machine that is used to send messages long distances through wires

Resources

Books

Thomas Alva Edison, Great Inventor
by Nancy Smiler Levinson
Scholastic (1996)

Thomas Alva Edison
by Brian Williams
Heinemann Library (2000)

Web Sites

Due to the changing nature of Internet links, PowerKids Press has developed an online list of Web sites related to the subject of this book. This site is updated regularly. Please use this link to access the list:

http://www.powerkidslinks.com/ncai/ite/

Index

Word Count: 403

Note to Librarians, Teachers, and Parents

If reading is a challenge, Reading Power is a solution! Reading Power is perfect for readers who want high-interest subject matter at an accessible reading level. These fact-filled, photo-illustrated books are designed for readers who want straightforward vocabulary, engaging topics, and a manageable reading experience. With clear picture/text correspondence, leveled Reading Power books put the reader in charge. Now readers have the power to get the information they want and the skills they need in a user-friendly format.